Want to Hear God?

Connect with Him in Prayer

Conversations That Transform Series

Nancy B. Booth

Abundant Grace
Publishers

Stoughton, WI

To Shelley and CJ, who shared God's prayers and
words with me so I could hear God say, "Share My prayers
with My people," and bring this book to completion.

To my dear friends who contributed
to and prayed for this book…

And to my readers whom I pray you hear God and Jesus say…
"But I have come to give you everything in abundance,
more than you expect—life in its fullness until you overflow!"
John 10:10b TPT

Contents

Foreword

Prayer. I thought I knew what it was.

I thought I knew my role in it, and truthfully, I thought the lukewarm results I was experiencing were all I would ever get.

But deep inside, I really hoped I was wrong.

So, five years ago when my well of self-sourcing ran dry, I finally stopped and asked Jesus to "teach me to pray." Then turning to Luke 11 to see what Jesus said to those who asked this same thing, I became fascinated by his simple response.

Jesus didn't really "teach" his disciples anything at all, at least not in the traditional sense. In other words, he didn't give them a long explanation *about* prayer or provide them with an extensive how-to manual.

Instead, Jesus invited them into a simple experience of prayer.

And in this powerful book, Nancy Booth does the same. She

takes your ordinary, walking-around-the-house, going-to-work, brushing-your-teeth-daily, I'm-having-a-bad-day life and pulls back the curtain so we can see the One who is always there, speaking, whispering; Emmanuel, the conversational, wants to be, "With-Us God."

Through engaging stories, timeless principles, and easy-to-implement practices this book will equip and encourage you to listen, speak to and hear from God in a deeper, more meaningful way.

He is vast. He is loving, and His power is limitless. So, let's get to know Him better. With your eyes wide open and heart expectant, join Nancy and join me.

Join the God-fueled movement of interactive prayer that is right now taking place around the globe.

You'll be glad you did!

Kim Avery, MA, PCC
Author of *The Prayer-Powered Entrepreneur: 31 Days to Building Your Business with Less Stress and More Joy.*[1]
Increase Influence. Impact. Income.
The Prayer-Powered Entrepreneur
Kim Avery Coaching | 863.326.6215

Introduction

When you co-write a book with God about hearing God speak, He gets to lead the way.

When I first started this book, I thought sharing the multiple ways God and I had connected in prayer over the years would be the subject matter. He has answered in many surprising ways. I wanted you to know His love and care.

Different prayer conversations changed the way I heard God speak to me.

I heard Him call me His beloved. I saw His hand leading me. I could actually sense His words in my very being.

However, as the book developed, it became clear, not only were my prayer

Different prayer conversations changed the way I heard God speak to me.

experiences to be shared, but others could share their prayer conversations, too. Transforming conversations happened as they heard God speak.

Interestingly enough, as I reflected on people's shared prayer conversations, I realized we don't often share what we hear from God. He wanted us to realize that people of all walks of life have connections with Him, not just me!

"Come and listen, everyone who reveres the True God, and I will tell you what He has done for me." Psalm 66:16

I use Bible verses throughout this book. I believe the Bible is God's way of sharing His specific love notes with us. I want to share His exact words with you so you can hear His voice.

"All of Scripture is God-breathed; *in its* inspired *voice, we hear* useful teaching, rebuke, correction, *instruction, and* training for a life that is right." 2 Timothy 3:16

Somehow in this current rational culture, it's okay to pray to God but seems unusual or weird to hear from God. I believe by reading the shared prayer conversations in this book you'll be able to detect a variety of ways God can and does speak. You will begin to hear and sense His presence in new and different ways.

Another intent of this book is to encourage you to share your own prayer conversations with others, especially your family and the next generation. God certainly encourages us to do that:

"As the word is passed along from parent to child. Babies not yet conceived will hear the good news—that God does what he says." Psalm 22:31 MSG

Ultimately, exploring the twelve prayer practices contained in this book can connect you with God and help you hear Him more clearly. Hearing and sensing His presence will bring abundance to your life.

Grace, peace, and love can alter your life and you will overflow to others. As you go through the practices, I hope you'll find ways

to make hearing God an everyday habit. Download your free journal (https://NancyBBooth.com/want-to-hear-god/) to help you record your conversations as you incorporate habits to make prayer connections and experience transformation.

He longs to speak to you and connect intimately.

How seeking God grew my prayer passion

My passion to seek God in prayer intensified on a weekend retreat with my friend Amy in the spring of 2015. I often suffered from migraines, depression, and anxiety, feeling like I couldn't get out of a dark room, bouncing off the walls, reeling in pain.

Amy suggested I attend a Christ-centered yoga retreat with her. Up until that time, I had not done much yoga, but something about the announcement drew me to retreat as if the Holy Spirit spoke directly to me. I knew I had to get to St Louis one way or another.

Amy agreed to drive the five hours to our retreat center that glorious spring weekend. As we neared St Louis, I saw the Arch in the distance, like a rainbow of promise. I wondered what promises God had in store for me.

Arriving at the beautiful retreat grounds that early spring day, the pines and carpet of green lawn, reminding me of Psalm 23, welcomed us. Amy and I settled into the inviting, comfortable retreat room. Small golden gift bags lay on our beds welcoming us. Inside, besides chocolate, we found individual scripture sayings, each different. My scripture read,

"Jesus (to the disabled man): Are you here in this place hoping to be healed?" John 5:6b

After reading it to Amy in amazement, I answered out loud, *"Why yes, as a matter of fact, I am!"*

My consent to Jesus opened the door to unbelievable healing that weekend. God met me intimately and personally.

During the retreat, we entered the yoga area as holy ground, no shoes, only bare feet, because God would meet us on our mats. And that He did.

God impressed on my heart:

"You are my daughter, whom I love."

"I hold you close to my chest, like a mother nurses a child" felt particularly meaningful since my own daughter sat nursing my grandson in my home at that moment.

"Touch my hem and you shall be healed."

"You are blessed to be a blessing."

"You are whole and healed."

My personal word, *whole,* became imprinted upon my heart from head to toe. Through story and the Word, He healed my self's wounded parts by His love and I became whole.

My insides shifted. I knew I walked away healed from depression that weekend. Could it be true? Healed in a moment? Yet in my heart of hearts, I knew what He had done. I walked around in wonder.

From that time on, He has continually shed light on me. The darkness of depression I had experienced previously has not returned. My passion for seeking and knowing Him continues to intensify.

In David Benner's book *Spirituality and the Awakening Self,* he writes,

> "The movement toward our true self in Christ would be impossible if healing were not a central part of this journey. But a developing relationship with Christ that includes prayer, the means of grace and participation in God's kingdom work of making all things new in Christ will always involve the healing and restoration of our true self."

I continue to live into the restoration of my true self through my listening conversations with God. Prayer changed my life and it can change yours.

I want that for you.

Look for God in the everyday prayer stories you are about to read. People like you have shared the sacred conversations they have had with God. They listened to God, had conversations, and came out differently. You can, too.

What prayer can do

In picking up a book about conversations with God, what are you hoping for? See if you identify with any of the following items.

Do you pray to:
- Understand He is there
- Get guidance and clarity
- Find pain relief
- Connect with God
- Transform your day
- Be assured you are on the right path
- Get peace
- Listen to Him speak
- Get an answer to your prayer
- Thank Him
- Ask for forgiveness
- Ask for help in issues facing family and friends
- Call out in grief
- Fix your family
- Wonder where He is
- Ask how much longer to wait
- Dissipate your anger
- Rest in Him
- Find your purpose
- Find change
- Look for hope

How many of these resonate with you? What would you add?

What this book provides

You will be reading the prayers of others who had real ongoing dialogues with God. After you read people's prayer conversations, pick and choose what practices you want to draw you closer to God. Remember to download your free journal (https://NancyBBooth.com/want-to-hear-god/).

This book does not presume a formula of dos and don'ts. You are the one to determine what will build your own close, personal relationship with God. You are the one to decide what habits you need to build in order to hear God well.

This book allows you to examine twelve different prayer practices to connect in an authentic relationship with God, so that you may hear God and experience transformation in your life.

The different ways of praying let you make intimate communication with God, Jesus, and the Holy Spirit. Determine as you listen and experiment with each practice how the prayers fit for you as you seek His heart. Your download journal will help you document your journey along the way. You will also experiment with what habits make it easier to incorporate new practices into your daily life.

May you receive His overflowing abundance in your life and release it to others around you.

As Jesus says:

"I came to give life with joy and abundance." John 10:10

That is my prayer for you—an intentional life of connection, joy, and abundance.

Blessings,

Nancy B Booth

Section One

Strengthen Your Present

Whationals it take to strengthen a friendship? Time together to communicate, the discovery of each other's likes and dislikes, or the wonder of united souls in silence?

What have strong friendships done for you in the past?

In this section, you'll discover four types of prayer that can strengthen you in your own day-to-day prayers. I want to introduce you to the people who have practiced these prayers. You'll get to listen in on their conversations with God in the following four practices: breath prayer, Lectio Divina, examen and centering prayer.

Breath Prayer

Strengthening your prayer relationship with God, Jesus, and

the Holy Spirit can be as close as your breath. You'll meet Amy as she discovered how God called her by name and strengthened her when practicing her breath prayer. You can learn this, too.

Lectio Divina

Experiencing Him through scriptures allows another way for you to strengthen your present day-to-day connection to God. Get a sense of His delight in you by learning Lectio Divina. Deanne shares how the Lectio prayer strengthened and changed her heart.

Examen

During hard times, in particular, talking over the day with God helps you realize how close or how far away you feel from Him. Cheri shows how the practice of Examen strengthens reflective muscles, curiosity, and sensing the presence of God.

Centering Prayer

The last practice to review for strengthening your friendship with God is centering prayer. Often times, being with a friend in silence is all you need to do. Observe Matt as he shares his real-time prayer of sitting with God with no words.

As you seek to strengthen your friendship with God on a more daily basis, I hope you'll find these first four practices provide a surprising warmth for you:
- Breath Prayer
- Lectio Divina
- Examen Prayer
- Centering Prayer

They are designed for connectedness and intimacy. God desires honest two-way conversations with you. The question is, *How can you get yourself in a place to hear Him speak and you are able to respond?*

Enjoy the authentic prayer conversations Amy, Deanne, Cheri, and Matt share with you. Then ponder the reflective questions following each prayer conversation as a way of pausing before moving into the prayer practice. Use your journal as a way to record your responses.

Finally, experiment on your own by exploring the prayer practice provided after each prayer conversation. Designed for you to listen and relate to God and yourself, the prayer practice provides a pathway for you to hear God and connect in prayer. Consider how you might incorporate these prayer practices into your day or week. Record those reflections in your journal (https:// NancyBBooth.com/want-to-hear-god/).

Also available to download are free scripture cards (https:// NancyBBooth.com/want-to-hear-god). They delineate scriptures used throughout this book. These cards will enhance your connection with God each day.

He will communicate with you. You can enjoy two-way conversations to strengthen your days. I am sure of it.

May I pray for you?
Father, out of Your honorable and glorious riches, strengthen Your people.
I ask that You fill each heart with the power of Your Spirit so that through faith
Jesus will reside in each heart.
I pray that each person may know love,
and that each one will have the power to understand that
the love of Jesus is infinitely long, wide, high, and deep,
surpassing everything anyone has experienced before.
God, may Your fullness flood each one through and through.
It is in Jesus' precious name, I pray,
Amen

Chapter 1

Being Present
Breath Prayer

"The same way a loving father feels toward his children—
that's but a sample of your tender feelings toward us, your
beloved children, who live in awe of you." Psalm 103:13 TPT

Amy

I return to breath prayer all the time.

My first experience with this kind of prayer happened in an unlikely place – a yoga class.

Our instructor asked us to, "Breathe in our name for God, and breathe out our need."

An example of that would be

Breathe in, Abba Father, breathe out, help me find peace.

Then continue to breathe those phrases as a prayer.

In the days and months to come, I found myself connecting with God through my breath.

A couple of years later I attended a Christ-centered yoga retreat where the theme was restoration and healing.

On our mats one morning, we were asked to settle in and find our breath prayer. After several minutes, the instructor asked us to switch the prayer around and listen for God's name for us and his response to our request.

I have never liked hearing my own name. It sounds small and unimportant to me. When there are other women in the room who share my name, I have always felt unseen.

After a few moments of silence, I heard God call me "Beloved" and with each breath, I felt God say, "I see you."

It was such a huge moment, especially when I realized that my name means "beloved" in Hebrew. I had a few goosebumps over that.

At that moment, I felt seen, and it was a very healing experience for me, something from my past that I felt like God just took and said,

"Amy, this is who you are, I see you, and this is my name for you. Amy, Beloved.

...and you need to learn to like it...

Embrace it."

That experience changed how I see myself. And helped me know that God truly sees me.

I am his Beloved.

The practice of breath prayer

The best thing about breath prayer is that I can do breath prayers while I am cooking dinner, or changing a baby's diaper. Whatever you are doing, God is right there.

You don't have to stop to do something intentionally. You can just take a breath and pray.

A breath prayer lets you sustain prayer without ceasing throughout your day. It helps me go back in remembrance with God, no matter what I am doing in my day.

God was there before. He is there now. He will be there for me and He sees me.

###

Questions to Ponder

1. What startled Amy at her retreat? God saw her. How and when have you realized that God sees you?
2. What time of day might work for you to start your exploration of breath prayer? Choose a time, decide how often, how to remember to pray, and begin now.
3. Draw three columns under this question or in your journal. Label the first column God, the second column Jesus, and the third column Holy Spirit. Now under each column write down different names that you may know. Examples are provided.

Under God: Lord, Jehovah, Abba, I AM

Under Jesus: Immanuel, Son of God

Under Holy Spirit: Counselor, Spirit of the Living God

Find other names by searching on Biblegateway.com or in a study Bible.

Which name(s) resonates with you? They can be ones you may wish to dig into deeper as you begin to practice breath prayers.

Action

Bring God's awareness as close to you as your breath. What do you need Him to whisper to you in the following prayer?

Breath Prayer

A brief in-and-out breath, with words attached to breathing. The repeated prayer, in those moments, allows focusing on who God is and what the participant desires from Him.

1. Sit comfortably, eyes closed or staring down, feet on the floor. Consider

    "Be still and know that I am God!" Psalm 46:10 NLT
2. Ask God to be present with you at this moment.
3. Breathe in and out several times gently.
4. Consider who is God to you at this moment:
    Immanuel
    God
    Father
    Abba
    Jesus
    Holy Spirit
5. Then decide what it is you would like to ask Him for:
    Bring peace
    Be with me
    Give mercy
    Show me hope

    Whatever is close to your heart at this moment.
6. On the inhale, pray God's name that you have chosen, such as Father God,
7. On the exhale, pray your request that you have chosen, such as Bring peace.
8. Continue praying that on your inhale and exhale, 7-8 times, slowly and focused on the words.
9. Rest. Become aware of how your mind, heart, and body reacted to this prayer.

10.   Thank Him and when ready, move back into your day.

Note: Maintain your same breath prayer daily or change the words over time. My breath prayer has remained the same for several months and is my go-to prayer.[2]

Chapter 2

Experiencing
Lectio Divina

"His wrap-around presence is all I need, for the Lord is my Savior, my hero, and my life-giving strength." Psalm 62:7 TPT

Deanne

Life can be so busy and hurried.

Lectio Divina[3] provides a way to slow down and step into a still space to hear God through His Word. This powerful practice leads me to deep and profound transformation as God uncovers lies I believe and replace them with His Truth.

I really love Lectio Divina. When I am participating in this prayer practice, it's almost like a slowing down. It is also, though, a fast track in terms of getting to the real root of where I am and meeting God there. When I practice Lectio Divina, my mind becomes still as I focus on Scripture and what the Holy Spirit is highlighting in my soul as I read and re-read.

The process allows me to notice and then unpack what God is whispering to my very being.

Suddenly the verses and truths move from my head to my heart and touch the deepest parts of me, changing how I observe and live in the world. Often, it is as if the spotlight shines on the extravagant love He has for me. The simplicity of saying yes to Him, allows Him to transform me from the inside out.

During Lectio Divina, I find answers to questions I didn't even realize I had.

God uses Lectio Divina to remove the barriers set up in my inner being, including the lies and false narratives lingering in my unconscious. The powerful peace of His presence replaces my striving and stress.

This spiritual practice has become something I look forward to, a profound way to experience God and allow His Truth to change me from the inside out.

This powerful practice, having practiced it for several months and participated in it on a regular basis, shows me how God transforms my life.

I am becoming aware of how present God is with me each day as well as how much He loves me.

Questions to Ponder

1. How does Deanne say God uses Lectio Divina to speak to her?
2. By practicing Lectio Divina, Deanne becomes informed of what differences in her life? What intrigues you about those changes Deanne discovers?

Action

Allow the practice of Lectio Divina to bring Scripture alive to you. How will God use it to speak to you?

Lectio Divina

A "divine reading" of Scripture that allows the reader to become immersed in the Scriptures with mind, heart, and soul. This allows the words to move from head knowledge to heart understanding.

1. For Lectio Divina, choose a passage of scripture, usually four to six verses. Proverbs 3:1–6 NLT can be the practice this time.

2. Grab a notebook or journal (or use the journal provided for you) in which to write down observations. Settle into the stillness. Ask God to help connect with Him.

3. "My child, never forget the things I have taught you. Store my commands in your heart. If you do this, you will live many years, and your life will be satisfying. Never let loyalty and kindness leave you! Tie them around your neck as a reminder. Write them deep within your heart. Then you will find favor with both God and people, and you will earn a good reputation. Trust in the LORD with all your heart; do not depend on your own understanding. Seek his will in all you do, and he will show you which path to take." Proverbs 3:1–6 NLT

4. Read the selection three times. Read it aloud and let the words wash over you.

5. **1st Reading:** Watch for a phrase or word to stand out to you as you read it. What resonates or "shimmers" for you? Reflect.

6. **2nd Reading:** Now look for things you are asked to do in

27

these verses. What is your role and or what impression do you get? Reflect.

7. **3rd Reading:** Now search for what God will do for you or what will be the result of trusting Him. Reflect.

8. After the three readings, **pause.** Ask God, "Of the things that stood out to me, God, how do You want me to move forward?" Take some time to meditate and visualize on what "shimmered" or was emphasized.

9. Thank Him for your time together.

Note: Psalms work well for Lectio Divina since they are prayers in and of themselves. Investigate Psalms 23, 34, 37, 42, 62, 90. Focus on small chunks of the passages at a time.

Use the scripture cards (https://NancyBBooth.com/want-to-hear-god) available to you to also meditate on His Word.

Chapter 3

Seeing
Examen

"You must each decide in your heart how much to give. And don't give reluctantly or in response to pressure. 'For God loves a person who gives cheerfully.'" 2 Corinthians 9:7 NLT

Cheri

In previous conversations with God when I would review the day using the practice of Examen[4] I noticed times when I was afraid to be generous. That would inspire me to ask God about my being generous to others.

Why can't I trust that I lack nothing in Him?

On this day, I had nothing special in mind as I sat down to pray. During that prayer, a moment from my childhood came to mind.

The scene, in my memory, took place during a time when my family had gone from financial security into extended financial insecurity. I could feel all the tension and angst in my family.

The abundant and full life we had known became long-lost with no apparent way out.

As I was sitting in the memory, it suddenly occurred to me this was an explanation for earlier requests of God on this topic.

The memory took me right back to all the same feelings of fear and despair that I experienced in those days. God allowed me to experience all the unique and powerful emotions of those particular days.

I sensed God bringing me something I needed to discern and had been asking to understand. I could clearly connect that beliefs formed at that moment long ago were keeping me from trusting the Lord now.

Seeing that connection between what I experienced in the past and my emotions now helped me let go of my unbelief. I could place my trust in what I understand now about God's generous heart.

God gave me hope that *believing in God's generous heart will be what I need in order to overcome my fears and respond to others with generosity, too.*

Examen becomes meaningful to me because I examine what is happening on a daily basis with a sense of compassion, grace, and curiosity. This way of praying prepares me to listen and receive what the Lord desires to give to me.

I've learned that the Lord answers my questions and longings over time, even though I may be asking Him the same thing each day. When I don't get a clear sign right away, I am not to get worked up or go striving.

The structure of the Examen gives me a place to record my questions so that I can be cognizant of His hand over time. It also gives me a place to go back to and think about what He is doing and has been doing.

The Examen also allows me to tell others what He is doing in my life.

More and more I find it important to find others I can share my prayer stories with and listen to their prayer stories as well.

When we share our conversations, God gets the glory and we are encouraged to listen and trust the process.

Questions to Ponder

1. Cheri recognized a pattern in her conversations with God when she was afraid to be generous. In your times with God, what reoccurring themes come up? What do you think God would like to reveal to you around those reoccurring themes?

2. In this Examen, God brought a memory to mind for Cheri, a type of pause, reflect, and remember. Often something in your past helps reveal something of God. How could that help your daily prayer time with God?

Action

As you practice Examen, you will notice where the presence of God feels close to you and when you notice you feel far from God. He doesn't move. Where would you like to hear, see and feel His presence in your life today?

Examen Prayer

A reflective prayer to review the day, detecting God's presence, noticing when you are aware of God's closeness and when you realize you feel distant from God.

1. Take time to settle before God. Choose the Examen in the evening to review your day or the next morning to review the previous day.

2. Reflect on the day, like running a movie camera throughout the day. Ask God to show where to stop the camera and zero in on certain scenes.

3. What happened that are you grateful for, even if it was an "unhappy" grateful, but are glad to realize something?

4. Where did you notice a feeling of closeness to God, feel His presence?

5. What drew you away from God, a feeling of distance from Him?

6. Ask God, "What part of my day am I to reconnect with?" Be curious about what He reveals. Talk with Him about that part.

7. What reflections and realizations about the day could you take into tomorrow? Thank Him for realizations.

Note: *Reimaging the Examen* app[5] for your phone may be something you wish to investigate. It gives you a variety of daily Examen themes from which to choose.

Chapter 4

Sensing
Centering Prayer

"Moses (to the Lord): Look, You tell me, 'Lead these
people!' but You haven't yet told me whom You will send to
accompany me. Yet You tell me, 'I know you by name, and
you have gained My trust and blessing.'" Exodus 33:12

Matt

Our church has a practice of inviting someone to pray with the people leading the worship and teaching teams before and after the Sunday services. On this given Sunday I covered both services.

I agreed to cover both but did not want to stay through the services so decided to go home during the first service. Instead of reading or watching the news, I sensed the Holy Spirit inviting me to use this time for centering prayer. This type of prayer, I realized, "trusts that being with Jesus brings transformation," as Adele Ahlberg Calhoun writes.[6]

I chose to follow the centering prayer method, seeking Christ's presence with my whole self. Quieting myself in a chair, I chose the word "Immanuel...God is with us." My thoughts would wander, but per the practice I would give myself grace and return to *Immanuel*, repeating and trusting that God was with me.

After a few minutes, I began to think of the church service that was happening as I was praying. My mind and heart began picturing all the different people who were part of our church family.

As I returned to the words "Immanuel...God is with us," Christ began transforming me. This change appeared as a deep sense of compassion for the many women in our church community who were alone in their struggles:

- Single mothers who had suffered great effort just to bring their children to church that morning
- Divorced mothers whose former husbands wanted nothing to do with supporting the faith of their children
- Widowers who were feeling so alone
- Women with addictions who were hoping for a strong male voice in their lives because they thought that would fix everything
- Women who were vanguards of prayer and faith who would do anything for their spouses to know of Jesus.

This was the Holy Spirit's revelation to me that morning. Prior to that point in time, I can honestly say I had not thought compassionately about this depth of need.

This prayer invited me into the transformational love that Jesus, and only Jesus, offers.

God sees people in ways that only an unveiling or revelation, an aligning with His kingdom, can offer us as humans.

In later discussions, when I shared this prayer conversation, I learned that others in the church with whom I work closely fit into these categories. Surprisingly to me, even two in the current Bible study group I was leading were covered by that prayer that morning. These two were not on my radar for the centering prayer, but God knew of their needs and brought that to my attention.

God will meet me in an intimate way when I turn my will toward Him and His glory. Centering prayer is a way that I can listen for His voice.

He will also bring ways I can pray for others as an encouragement.

Questions to Ponder
1. Centering prayer is seeking *Christ's presence with my whole self* as Matt writes. When have you had this type of experience with Jesus and the Holy Spirit? What was it like?
2. If you haven't prayed using centering prayer, what makes you curious about Matt's listening to God using this type of prayer? What are you wondering?
3. How could centering prayer help you listen for God's voice and how God may be at work around you?

Action
Centering prayer can bring you peace. Where could you practice this prayer?

Centering Prayer
A time of meditation with God, letting silence wash over you, listening to hear what He reveals. It is based on a relationship with God, through Christ, letting Him direct your thoughts.

1. Sit down in a solitary place. You might want to start with 5 minutes and work up to 15–20 minutes. Use of a timer is recommended so you're not worried about the time. Or you may choose to download the *Centering Prayer*[7] app from Contemplative Outreach as a tool in which you can choose the length of time. Remember, the Spirit's "got you."

2. Choose a sacred word(s) as the symbol to consent to God's presence and action in you. You may even want a word from a short verse of scripture. "You will keep in perfect peace all who trust in you" (Isaiah 26:3 NLT). It symbolizes the consent of your will toward Him within you as well as His actions.

3. Sit comfortably with eyes closed. Settle in. Breathe easily. After a few moments of not doing anything, casually introduce the sacred word(s).

4. When engaged with thoughts, turn to your chosen word. Acknowledge the fact you will find distractions. Noises, thoughts, etc., are inevitable, integral, and normal. Don't resist them. Thomas Keating says to "have a joyful, friendly attitude toward them. Receive them with a smile." Return to the sacred word(s) when you find distractions.

5. This is a time of "being" in God's presence. You don't need to "do" anything. Continually return to your "sacred word" as an opportunity to sit in silence with God, letting go of all the thoughts and chatter in your mind. He is within you and meeting Him in the silence is the practice.

6. Take a couple of minutes to come out of prayer. Don't hurry. Breathe in the presence of Christ.

7. Reflect upon what is on your mind, heart, and body as you come out of the prayer. What is the same or different from when you started?

Section 2

Redeem and Restore Your Past

When you think about redeeming something, what do you consider? Buying or getting it back, such as redeeming coupons? Jesus came to redeem us and free us from what distresses or harms us, such as sin.

In today's world, many people recoil from the word *sin*, but in reality, the word *sin* means "missing the mark." I think you would agree that in our lives we easily "miss the mark." Baggage from years before interferes with the life you want to live now.

Jesus frees you and me from our past because of God's plan of redemption. You and I can be free from shame, guilt, past mistakes by believing in Jesus.

"It's the word of faith that welcomes God to go to work and set things right for us. This is the core of our preaching. Say the welcoming word to God—'Jesus is my Master'—embracing, body and soul, God's work of doing in us what he did in raising Jesus from the dead. That's it. You're not 'doing' anything; you're simply calling out to God, trusting him to do it for you. That's salvation. With your whole being, you embrace God setting things right, and then you say it, right out loud: 'God has set everything right between him and me!'" Romans 10:8–10 MSG

Have you set everything right between you and God by believing in Jesus? If you are not sure, check on "Welcoming Jesus Into Your Life" in the appendix. Confirm indeed you are free because of Jesus. Jesus is your bridge to God.

In section 2, you'll find practices that redeem your past and restore, free, and heal you. Let go of things that interfere with your communication and connection with God and with others.

The four redeeming and restorative prayer practices for you to explore include:

Confession Prayer

In the confession prayer, you'll find Nancy surrendering her need to control the life of her adult daughter, especially in crisis times. God showed her many things, including a vision of His concern for her daughter. Nancy found she needed to trust Him. You'll glimpse how the prayer of confession can bring peace to your soul.

Lament Prayer

Rayna shares how her miscarriage losses drove her away from God. She realized those losses colored her view of God. Lamenting and giving God her emotions allowed her to let go and heal again. He, too, gave her a vision. You can find the practice of lament valuable as you grieve the loss of people, places, or events.

Imaginary Prayer

In this type of prayer, you will use your mind's eye to put yourself into the actual scriptural passage. By practicing this type of prayer, you may discover what Jesus wants to reveal and heal in you. You'll follow Sheri's journey to the temple with Jesus and His clearing of the money lenders. He had things to tell her about herself during that communication time with Jesus.

Silence and Solitude

Jesus often drew away from the crowds and calls you and me to do that as well. Being quiet with God brings much soothing and intimacy as He refreshes our whole being. As Jeff shares, no words needed. Listening in the stillness, like sitting with your best friend, reveals peace to the soul, as you lean into God.

As you seek to redeem and heal your past, these next four prayer practices may provide tools that begin a healing process for you.

- Confession Prayer
- Lament Prayer
- Imaginary Prayer
- Silence and Solitude

As you practice the prayers, notice the freedom, authenticity, and restoration that begin to emerge. He desires you to be whole and healed, released from chains of the past. He looks at you as if you never sinned. Grace becomes a gift of unmerited favor, and He holds it out to you.

After each story, you can redeem your own past with God and Jesus by practicing the prayers for your specific situations. Journaling becomes particularly important as you revisit the past. You also may want to find a trusted friend or spiritual director to accompany you in these prayer practices of redemption and healing.

Go slow and lean into Jesus with these practices. Ask Him to direct your prayers and let you see where He was with you in your past. If these practices are not for now, there may be a time later. Attach yourself to practices that bring healing, wholeness, and redemptive prayer conversations with Him.

He will speak to your heart. I am sure of it.

May I pray for you?

Lord God,

Thank You that You pursue us and want a restored and healthy relationship between us.

I pray that each of us looks to You for healing, redemption, and wholeness.

You do not hold our sins against us, but through Jesus, You heal and restore our broken relationships with You and each other.

May we seek You with all of our hearts, minds, and souls to receive what You have to offer.

Thank You for making us healed and whole.

Amen

Chapter 5

Surrendering
Confessional Prayer

"God, give me mercy from your fountain of forgiveness!
I know your abundant love is enough to wash away
my guilt. Because your compassion is so great, take
away this shameful guilt of sin." Psalm 51:1-2 TPT

Nancy

I had been thinking, thinking, thinking about what to share with
my adult daughter.

Her non-existent on-site hair and make-up business
for weddings needed a financial infusion. The pandemic had
decimated her income. My own thinking contained many helpful
details from the news. I believed I had the knowledge to share with

her. As a single mom, my daughter had her hands full with rent to pay and an active six-year-old son.

Since sleep was elusive, I furiously journaled my thoughts and feelings to God, crying my heart out to Him. He then brought to my mind a recent *Unlocking Us* podcast by Brené Brown.

The podcast featured people in families that either over-function or under-function, especially during times of anxiety and uncertainty. The over-functioning person takes on responsibilities they don't need, in an effort to make everything better.

The under-functioning people sit back, play, and feel the victim. They let other people take the lead while feeling lost and incompetent. These under-functioning souls tend to feel "less than" by the person in charge.

"Again, as over-functioning people, we tend to move very quickly to advise, rescue, takeover, basically get in other people's business rather than looking at what's going on inside. Under-functioning people tend to get less competent under that stress and they often invite people to take over. And often not only do they invite people to take over, but in addition to whatever is causing the stress and anxiety, they become the focus of more stress and anxiety. On the outside as over-functioning, we can appear to be very tough and in control. And sometimes the under-functioning can appear to be irresponsible or even fragile."[8]

God began tapping me on the shoulder.

"Who is over-functioning in your family and who is under-functioning?"

Wow! Talk about hitting me between the eyes. Over-functioning, being judgmental, controlling, and prideful described me to a T. "I am the one to know best." The necessity of surrendering my control, worry, and anxiety over my adult daughter to Him became quite apparent.

God reminded me of a vision He had given me several years back. In it, my daughter and her son, sit happily on Jesus' lap, laughing. Jesus had his arms around them and they were well cared for.

"What part of this vision of care and provision that I showed you before don't you trust, Nancy?"

I humbly asked God's forgiveness for not trusting Him and confessed this sin, this "missing the mark." As I made this confession, a great load lifted immediately from my shoulders.

In addition to confessing, God prompted me to write a letter to my daughter. I asked her forgiveness for me not trusting her to regulate her own affairs. I let her know I would always be her biggest fan and support her however I could. From this day forward, I would stop with the advice and meddling.

What a difference in my whole being after surrendering everything over to God as well as asking for forgiveness. I found I had much more headspace. Instead of my mind full of worry, I could write freely on my book. No longer responsible for her life, I could focus on what was mine to do, and God would take care of her.

In surrender, I could acknowledge God's tender mercies new every morning. He erased my guilt and shame. I knew I could trust Him.

He was the one in charge. What a blessed change!

Questions to Ponder

1. Wanting to "fix" things for her daughter, Nancy lost sleep over the situation she felt was hers to solve. Has that happened to you? How did you cry out to God and what happened?

2. Nancy took her situation to God and recognized surrender was key because she was missing the mark. When has God revealed to you a time when you were doing something for someone that wasn't yours to do? How did you resolve it?

3. Understanding what to confess and who she needed to ask forgiveness from—both God and her daughter—became clear to Nancy as she listened to God. Who does God bring to mind that you may need to ask forgiveness from? A parent? A partner? A child? A friend? Take time and ask Him, "Lord, bring to mind who or what I need to confess."

Action

Where and with whom are you "missing the mark"? Consider that person who weighs heavy on your mind as you take this opportunity to become free.

Confessional Prayer[9]

An opportunity to bring your missteps and wrongdoings, those times of "missing the mark" (sin), before God, asking for forgiveness and making a new start.

1. Get silent before God.
2. Come before Him, seeing His eyes of softness and mercy.
   "God, give me mercy from your fountain of forgiveness! I know your abundant love is enough to wash away my guilt. Because your compassion is so great, take away this shameful guilt of sin." Psalm 51:1-2 TPT
3. Unite with God with a humble and softened heart, asking Him what to confess. Pause. What does He bring to mind?
4. Describe the burden that is heavy on your heart, the one you want to surrender to Him. What do you want to release to Him?
5. Ask *Where am I missing the mark?*
6. You may think you are cognizant, yet He may reveal more.
7. Making your confession, you agree with His revelation.
8. Repent or "turn away from" what you confessed.

9. Ask God for a description of His character to hold on to as you let go of this sin. Trust, love, courage, strength. Even ask for an object as a remembrance — a rock, a white blanket, something concrete.
10. Receive and rejoice over His forgiveness.
11. Notice the difference in your body between when you came into the prayer and at the end. Where were you carrying your burden when entering your prayer time?
12. In confession, according to the Scriptures, God:
    - Cleanses
    - Heals
    - Forgives
    - Responds
    - Restores
13. What was your experience? What will you remember?

Chapter 6

Grieving
Lament

"I'm hurting, Lord—will you forget me forever?
How much longer, Lord? Will you look the other
way when I'm in need? How much longer must I
cling to this constant grief?" Psalm 13:1-2 TPT

Rayna

My whole life I have always wanted to be a mom.

When I married my second husband at thirty-nine, I was hopeful this life-long dream could come true and we would have children. Two and a half years into our marriage, I got pregnant. I was so excited.

Immediately, I started dreaming of what it would be like to raise this baby with my husband on the farm. I was so sick but I was so happy. As the weeks went by, I finally started to feel less sick.

At twelve weeks we had our first sonogram only to find out I was less sick because the twins were no longer alive. Devastated, I grieved and grieved the loss of my beautiful babies. I grieved all the things I wanted to share with them and the loss of the badge of honor, being called mom.

The doctor was hopeful we would get pregnant again soon, but it didn't happen. Each month, I grieved the babies I had lost and struggled with God in the why. The longer this went on the less I would talk with God about having kids.

I felt so overlooked.

I felt as if God didn't care how important being a mom was to me.

A few years later, I found myself struggling with asking God for anything. He had not answered the desire of my heart, why would he answer other things that are not as important to me?

I was sharing with a friend one day about how I was struggling with this. She said, "Let's stop and talk with Him about it now."

Then she asked me to put my finger on what I was believing about God that wasn't true. Immediately the word *cruel* came to mind. It felt cruel for God to allow me to get pregnant but then take my babies away from me.

I knew in my head that God wasn't cruel, but I couldn't figure out how to feel any other way about it. She then asked me to ask God to show me where I was wrong.

When I said, "Lord, help me to see how getting pregnant but not having my kids here isn't cruel," He showed me a vision of Jesus with my son sitting on his lap.

He said, *"Rayna, but you are a mom. Your kids are right here with Me."*

Then I saw my mom walk to Jesus with my baby girl in her arms.

"They are here waiting for you to spend eternity with them."

As tears streamed down my face, peace settled over my heart. I still struggle with not being a mom of kids here on this earth, but now I never feel overwhelmed by it.

I know God is not cruel. There is peace still today, knowing I will spend eternity with my kids.

Being willing to lament that which hurts about this life led me to peace. I told God exactly how I felt. I then learned to ask for a new perspective since I am not always right, nor can I view the whole picture. He is God and He oversees things perfectly.

He wants me to remember who He is and that He loves me.

He is willing to talk with me about anything, anytime.

###

Questions to Ponder

1. What was keeping Rayna from feeling close to God? What in your life keeps you from feeling close to God?
2. What did Rayna go through in her lament to get closer to God again?
3. What might you need to be willing to take to God and ask for healing and a new perspective?

Action

Bring all your sorrows, pain, and grief authentically to God as honestly as you can as you explore the lament.

Lament Prayer[10]

A prayer crying out to God with all emotions, telling Him like it is, and focusing on who He is while grieving or in pain.

1. What is weighing heavy on your heart? Grief, pain, forgiveness? Take time to ask God to help you clarify what you want and need to bring before Him. Use the scripture

after each point below.

2. Address God—How do you address God? What do you comprehend about His nature or character that could bring you help in your situation?

"I'm hurting, Lord—will you forget me forever? How much longer, Lord? Will you look the other way when I'm in need?" (Psalm 13:1 TPT).

3. Call out your complaint—What is your struggle, disappointment, crisis, or situation that requires God's attention? God welcomes our honest cries.

"Take a good look at me, God, and answer me! Breathe your life into my spirit. Bring light to my eyes in this pitch-black darkness or I will sleep the sleep of death" (Psalm 13:3 TPT).

4. Ask Him—What do you desire God to do on your behalf? Tell him where you are and explain to Him where you need His help.

"Lord, I have always trusted in your kindness, so *answer me*" (Psalm 13:5a TPT).

5. Affirm God—What can you affirm about God? Where has He helped you in the past? What have you experienced to be true and good about Him?

"I will yet celebrate with passion and joy when your salvation lifts me up" (Psalm 13:5b TPT).

6. Close in praise/gratitude—Can your lament end in praise? Is there anything you can be thankful for? How about a vow to not give up on God or yourself until you come through this difficult season? Make an agreement to wait on His provision, timing, deliverance, and justice.

"I will sing my song of joy to you, the Most High, for in all of this you have strengthened my soul" (Psalm 13:6 TPT).

7. Tell someone—A lament always kept to yourself can lead to despair or isolation.[11]

Chapter 7

Healing
Imaginary Prayer

"Jesus: *What are you still doing here?* Get all your stuff,
and haul it out of here! Stop making My Father's house a
place for your own profit! *The disciples were astounded*, but
they remembered that the Hebrew Scriptures said, 'Jealous
devotion for God's house consumes me.'" John 2:16–17

Sheri

I engaged with Jesus in an imaginary journey through the
Ignatian Exercises.[12]

These exercises created by St. Ignatius of Loyola, the founder
of the Jesuits, invite you and me to an opportunity to use your
imagination. Based on scripture, you can pray and "see" with the

eyes of your heart and place yourself into the scenes of the Bible.

When I arrived in the Jewish temple in my mind, it was during Lent, a time before the crucifixion of Jesus. I was in a prayerful state, using my imagination, as Jesus invited me to "go up the steps" to the temple with Him. I went into His "Father's House" from John 2:16–17.

As a pilgrim in the Exercises, I was seeking to learn from Jesus and glean from how He lived out his life, the remaining portion of life here on earth. There I was watching. Jesus just flew into what seemed like a tantrum to me. As you read the above verses, you uncover how unhappy Jesus was with the people in the temple.

Now, usually, I run and hide from these kinds of events.

I found myself hunkered way down in a corner of the temple as far away as I could get from the action.

I began to feel "guilty" for not helping, worthless for not being more present for Jesus and so inadequate as a follower of His!

My head voices started whispering.

Why aren't you helping him? You should be doing…! You should know better; you know the story!

As I reflected on myself in the scene, I could perceive how I had been very much myself in those moments. I was ashamed of my lack of behavior and wished I had done much more!

So, after using my imagination, I took time for prayer and reflection as part of the process of this imaginary prayer practice.

Jesus called me to a "come to Jesus" meeting!

I was somewhat stoic and thought I had my confession to Jesus well-prepared! We went in my mind's eye to the hillside above the Sea of Galilee for our time together.

> Jesus connected to my heart like He connected to the heart of the Samaritan woman, "He told me everything I ever did!" (John 4:39 NLT).

After some uncomfortable silence, He began to speak. He began by encouraging me not to berate myself, but to accept myself with all the unique ways Abba Father created me.

He said, *"Sheri, please know that your quiet and prayerful presence in a time like that is equally as important as what I did. I need people like you.*

"You will continue to learn how best to use the gifts within you to help others along the journey. For now, let's be thankful together for those moments and for your willingness to have the courage to live into who you are and how you'll live out your life!

"Then you will always have the full life that I came to bring!"

This particular prayer has stuck with me. I revisit it whenever I need to remember to accept myself with all the unique ways Abba Father created me.

Thank you, Abba Father, for the gift of imaginary prayer. Amen

###

Questions to Ponder

1. Engaging your imagination when reading the Scriptures is not making something up. You can picture someone you care about in your mind's eye. As you visualize Sheri's recounting of Jesus in the temple, what can you imagine that scene was like? What could it be like for you if you had been there?

2. How might engaging your imagination with Jesus help you *learn from Jesus and glean from how* He lived out his life, the remaining portion of life here on earth? What did you appreciate about Sheri's time with Jesus?

Action

Explore using your imagination to get to know, see, and hear Jesus better.

Imaginary Prayer[13]

Engaging with imagination as a place to enter into where you can envision Jesus and discover His embrace of love and healing presence.

1. When you get ready to use your imagination, it may not be what you think it is. It is not pretending or making up something that is not true as you meet with Jesus. For example, picture for a moment, someone who is special to you. Try to imagine that person vividly, with color, details, even placing them in the last place you saw them. Are you making them up or recalling to mind someone who is alive and real?

2. The same is true as you read the scenes in the Bible, asking God to help you perceive the details He has picked out for you. You are envisioning the story so it becomes real to you, and therefore Jesus becomes real as well.

3. The Gospels are a great place to become acquainted with Jesus. The first imaginary prayer framework we will visit focuses on Mary and Martha, Luke 10:38–42 NIV. You will read it through three times aloud, with a different emphasis each time. A Bible version on your phone where you can listen to NIV Dramatized[14] can be advantageous.

4. Get comfortable and ask God to help you envision the scene with your mind's eye. You may want your journal nearby to catch some of the vividness of this imaginative journey.

5. Read through or listen to the following passage with your senses, noticing the sights, sounds, smells, touches, even tastes. What provokes you in this story? What are you noticing about Jesus' humanity?

"As Jesus and his disciples were on their way, he came to a village where a woman named Martha opened her home to him. She had a sister called Mary, who sat at the Lord's feet listening to what he said. But Martha was distracted by all the preparations that had to be made. She came to him and asked, 'Lord, don't you care that my sister has left me to do the work by myself? Tell her to help me!'

'Martha, Martha,' the Lord answered, 'you are worried and upset about many things, but few things are needed—or indeed only one. Mary has chosen what is better, and it will not be taken away from her'" (Luke 10:38-42 NIV).

6. Pause to imagine. What did you notice?
7. Now be ready to read through or listen to the above passage in Luke again. This time as you read it, put yourself in the scene. How does this story intersect with your story?
8. Pause to imagine. What are the intersections of your story with Mary and Martha?
9. This third time reading or listening, listen with the eyes of your heart. When a thought comes to you, does it sound like Jesus speaking to you?
10. Take a few moments of silence to take in all that Jesus said to you. You may want to jot down notes in your journal or draw a picture.
11. What are you taking away from this imaginary encounter with Jesus?

Chapter 8

Resting
Silence and Solitude

"The LORD is my shepherd; I have all that I need.
He lets me rest in green meadows; he leads me
beside peaceful streams." Psalm 23:1–2 NLT

Jeff

A t the beginning of my relationship with God, I thought
prayer was mostly about saying the right words to God.
Perhaps, like a new couple just starting to date, they try
to impress and woo one another, afraid of the silence. It's all about
the right words.

In the early days of marriage, I remember seeing older couples
at a restaurant who hardly spoke, and I insisted we'd never want to

be like that. Now I perceive there is beauty and intimacy in being together in one another's presence without needing words.

I've discovered God meets me consistently in silence and solitude.

For me, I have found the best way for silence and solitude is to take only my Bible and myself and get away to a different location. Sometimes, it may take a while to decompress from the busyness of work and the world around me so I can respond to His voice.

Since I cannot leave home often during this period of the pandemic, silence and solitude are more challenging. I take time to unplug from technology, spend time in the garden, and be outdoors as I seek Him to refresh my soul in silence and solitude.

I find Him ready to encourage, lift, remind, redirect, or empower me. My role is to pause my words and activity long enough, even a noticeable moment, to attune to His still voice.

Psalm 23 allows me to seek God's care and presence in silence. I've returned to this Psalm often, reading and re-reading, then sitting in the quiet and inviting God to engage with me.

There's no formula or guaranteed outcome to this. Sometimes it's no reply. Sometimes I receive a clear impression of God's love and concern.

Just "being" with God, without needing to say anything, produce anything, accomplish anything is a gift. It's a reminder that He loves me as I am.

Discovering that words aren't necessary for meaningful connections has been a transformative part of my prayer life.

Simply being with God in silence and solitude is good and life-giving.

Questions to Ponder

1. How do you experience silence and solitude? How does Jeff describe it?

2. What happens when, as you sit in the stillness with someone else, and no words are needed? What could you experience in a situation like that?
3. What would it take to get more regular silence and solitude into your life? What benefits might you enjoy?

Action

Choose a place and time now when you can get quiet with God.

Silence and Solitude

Moving into places and spaces to be curious and wonder about the mystery of meeting God without words.

Dallas Willard says "*that the way to liberation and rest is through a decision and a practice — the decision to release the world and your fate into the hands of God through the radical practice of solitude and silence.*"[15]

What would it look like to get some silence and solitude in your life?

This verse exemplifies our experience often:

"This is what the Sovereign LORD, the Holy One of Israel, says: 'In repentance and rest is your salvation, in quietness and trust is your strength, but you would have none of it'" (Isaiah 30:15 NIV).

Here is one way to search out silence and solitude:

1. Choose a time when you can be by yourself without interruption. It might be on a walk, a time to journal in your office, on the front porch of your home, or even in your garden.
2. The point is you are not talking to anyone. You're putting yourself in a listening mode.
3. If you are not in a place of reading your Bible, ask God for one verse to meditate on while you walk or sit.

4. Write it on a card if the verse is not memorized or use the free scripture cards provided if you'd like to do so (https://NancyBBooth.com/want-to-hear-god/). The main point is to allow God's Word to reflect through your thoughts.

5. If you are sitting, ask Him for scripture to meditate on, or try the following:

    Psalm 23

    Psalm 46:10-12

    Isaiah 55

    Matthew 5:3-12 MSG

    Matthew 11:28-30 MSG

6. Then take the time to listen and be quiet. Bask in the stillness.

7. Take a rest, nap, relax…whatever you need to do to get some downtime with God. Let the silence and solitude wash over you.

8. Ask when sitting or walking with God, *"What is on Your heart for me today, God?"*

9. At the end of your time, thank God for your time together and ask Him for a word or symbol of remembrance to take away with you.[16] Make note of it in your journal.

Section 3

Transform Your Future

When you think about transforming your future, what comes to mind? Is it yours to change? Yet, you dream with hopes, desires, and wants. You want to move forward for yourself, for others, and even for the world. God desires to unite Himself with those things in your heart.

Transformation often becomes more apparent as you reflect backward. You recognize God's hand as He has made changes in your character, your condition, or your answered prayers in ways you would have never dreamed.

That's why prayer conversations with Him are powerful and transformative because, even before your eyes, changes occur. You get a thought you realize didn't come from you, a view of something you would have never seen before. You sense being carried along by loving forces.

As you detect more of His presence, you can be His hands and feet to transform not only your future but the future of others. Each of us is called to be a distributor of God's love, not change agents. That is God's job. You and I get to join Him in whatever He is doing.

Several prayer practices enhance opportunities to participate with God. Those practices include:

Gratitude Prayer

Gratitude prayer lets you and me be aware of where God is in our own lives and in the lives of the people around us. Mary's journey into praise and gratitude with God includes being thankful for even the tough stuff.

Scriptural Prayer

Not sure what or how to talk to God in prayer? Words of Scripture can help frame your prayers. Ruthmari retells how Scripture permeates her thinking. It has lovingly carried her through isolation times. God gave her joy when her first reaction would have been a complaint.

Intercessory Prayer

One prayer practice to develop may be asking God who to pray for each day. Perhaps there are specific people He has for you to hold up. Mark shares how running clears his mind and allows God to bring certain people to mind or things he is to do to encourage others. Those prayers become ways of distributing Jesus' love.

Believers' Prayer

Seeing and knowing a bigger God, as Creator of Heaven and Earth and Sovereign lets you know that God goes before you to guide the way.

Nancy tells how God led her to serve others at InterVarsity's Urbana conference. God led the way after nudging her to seek out one specific person who needed encouraging prayer.

When you desire to transform the future with God and become intimate with Him, I hope you'll find these last four practices transforming:

- Gratitude Prayer
- Scriptural Prayer
- Intercessory Prayer
- Believers' Prayer

They become revelations of who and what He introduces to your mind and heart. You may begin to see the results of those prayers. He wants you to distribute His love to others. You literally reconstruct the future with your prayers by sharing His love with others.

After each story, practice the prayers and find opportunities to distribute His love. Become curious about what practices fit you and, again, record those observations in your journal. Where are conversations becoming more and more real to you?

May I pray for you?

Lord Jesus,

You know what our hearts need. We desire and long for intimacy with You that will change our hearts and make us more like You.

Continue to draw us closer to You so that we see where You are at work and delight in the joy of walking with You.

Transform us to be more like You.

We want to be Your hands and feet.

Thank You, Jesus, for that privilege.

Amen

Chapter 9

Praising
Gratitude

"Let joy be your continual feast. Make your life a prayer. And in the midst of everything be always giving thanks, for this is God's perfect plan for you in Christ Jesus." 1 Thessalonians 5:16–18 TPT

Mary

I started a gratitude journal challenge a year ago and it has changed how I process my world.

The gratitude journal challenge started from the book *Make Miracles in Forty Days* by Melody Beattie.[17] In it, she challenges the reader to turn what you have into what you want by writing daily that for which you are grateful.

Three things set this challenge apart from any other gratitude list-making I had heard about before:

1. I was to set goals for myself for the next forty days that were near to my heart. I could keep those things in mind as I wrote down the grateful things.

2. My gratitudes were to be for everything, such as "I am grateful that I am so exhausted from all the work today. I am thankful, though, that the work is completed." It's not just I am grateful for my family, today. It's noticing the hard stuff, too, of negotiating how to get along.

3. I am to have an accountability partner who reads what I write but doesn't comment on it. By having a partner, I am more likely to keep writing.

Often, for me, going over an issue that happened, reexamining it out of that time and space allows me to recognize gratitude. I listen to what lesson I am to learn. Did I respond with my gut? Was I being rational? Was I responding out of my own guilt?

Journaling has been recommended to me. I'd never had success in sticking with it until I had a commitment to another person to exchange journals back and forth. Additionally, I had payback for me because I got to find out what's happening in my friend's life. That commitment keeps me writing.

Sometimes when I dig into the writing, it's okay this is what was going on. Sometimes, it is a catharsis of I was so angry and putting that to rest in an appropriate space rather than being angry at all people. I am grateful I have a place and space to record my feelings on paper and turn them over to God.

God listens and leans into me as I process my gratitude and thinking.

What I like about this gratitude practice is being grateful for even what I don't like. For example, I am not grateful for how my husband practices his faith, which is different from what I do. Yet God reminds me it is an experience of life. I can process the parts

I am grateful for, like he actually believes in God.

Some of the resistance to journaling is an emotional reaction to what occurred. I am to allow myself space before I can write it again. Other times when I write, nothing much has happened. That's okay, too. It makes me feel good for I have not missed reflecting on a day, yet. I am not sure I would have been able to develop the attitudes and revelations from God unless I had written down the gratitudes.

Sometimes the goals I write down are met and sometimes they are not. In a way, the goals are secondary, like icing on the cake. I realize I don't have to be so goal-oriented.

God will move when He will move.

For me, these gratitudes are a clarification process and a way to experience the world differently. This transformative process keeps me looking at the world through an authentic lens with God at my side.

I am praising God and grateful.

Questions to Ponder
1. What is different to you about this method of looking at gratitude? How could this way be valuable?
2. How could recording gratitude in this way aid you in listening to God?
3. Who might be an accountability partner to help you examine gratitude in this way? What might change in your life if you had someone to go with you on this "gratitude journey"?

Action
Call or email someone right now to join you on your gratitude journey. It will make such a difference to have someone come alongside you.

Gratitude Prayer

Expressing appreciation, thanksgiving, and acknowledgment to God in prayer, regardless of the circumstances.

As you get ready to approach this gratitude challenge prayer time, consider the following:

1. Who could you invite to go on this journey with you? Ask God to reveal someone you might ask to be your partner.

2. To start the forty-day challenge, take time to write down your hopes, dreams, and reflections for the next forty days. Where would you like **to be** in forty days? What would you like **to do**? What would you like **to have**? Give all these to God as you offer them up in gratitude.

3. Recruit someone as your accountability partner. Determine how you will participate with each other in getting your gratitudes back and forth. Email can work well.

4. Take a moment each day to jot down your gratitudes. Write in bullets, phrases, sentences, whatever works for you. Dictating it into your phone as audio could even be a choice, too.

5. For example:

   Today I am grateful for:

   Realizing I need more of a plan for my morning routine before breakfast. Scrolling through Facebook is not beneficial and/or reading the day's headlines is making me anxious so I am glad I realize that.

   Another morning of a routine, reading Scriptures and journaling, so helpful to start the day more connected to God and more productive.

6. However, if you miss a day or two, don't worry. Take the time to go back if you can. Reflecting gratitudes is more important

in hindsight than missing a day. Make the commitment to not miss days. He will bring to remembrance what is necessary.

7. Ask God to show you the things in which you can be appreciative, thankful for, or acknowledge His work in your life, even if in a challenging circumstance. What may God be teaching you, showing you?

8. Make a quick bullet list or paragraph of what God is revealing to you.

9. Send it to your gratitude partner.

10. Thank God for His revelations for the day.

11. Keep going!

12. After forty days, review and compare to your be, do, have goal list. Where did God show up these last days for you?

13. Start over.

Chapter 10

Asking
Scriptural

"Let the morning bring me word of your unfailing love,
For I have put my trust in you. Show me the way I should
go, for to you I entrust my life." Psalm 143:8 NIV

Ruthmari

S cripture reading in the morning informs my day.
It puts a filter on my eyes and on how I observe things throughout the day. The scriptures I am reading currently are on photo cards and focus on the overarching concepts of gratitude, peace, and rest. Not rest like take a nap, but rest like don't worry, chill, God's got this.

Each one of those different scriptures says it in a different way but informs the way I view the world every day. The conversation with God happens as I observe different parts of nature and creation.

I thank Him for the wonder, beauty, and intricacies of His world.

I live on five beautiful acres in southern Wisconsin. To look around, He is everywhere in nature. Living on the farm makes me live with my eyes open. The scriptures help me be able to view His presence and wonder. I am stuck in the natural world as spring unfolds.

The natural world is my current focus. Even in what I am making, as a creative, in my pottery, my photography, my jewelry-making. Yes, it's even in what I am drawing, e.g. poppies on my ceramics, all this natural world influencing me. Yes, it is coming out everywhere. I like it a lot.

Seeing the world through His eyes and being here on the farm, soaking in the natural world settles my soul. I am settled, as I have always wanted. Being with the God I have always known and been very comfortable with, yet there is this wonder. He's given me big eyes and exploration and discovery. This wonder takes ahold of the creative side of me and inspires me to do other things.

It's not that I want to do anything differently. That's another discovery. Lots of doing is going on. Planning and getting the garden beds ready, weeding the flower beds, mowing, feeding and care of the chickens, lots to do outside but it's not doing. How does that even work? I feel like I am being a farmer, and I say farmer loosely. I am a tender of this space that God has given us.

What I am doing is working the land, but I am being who He wants me to be at this moment.

So what I discovered is, I'm living a be and a do at the same time. The good thing about that discovery is that we are not required to do anything different tomorrow. So, if all the work doesn't get done today, we will move ahead with it tomorrow.

No big urgency to get all these to-dos done. We aren't leaving in two weeks or think we'll be gone for a month. We don't need to worry. We're certainly are not going anywhere.

So, I work at what is in front of me, with God's words running through my head.

When I am tired, or it's dinner time, or whatever, I stop. Then the next day, I pick up where I left off and it doesn't matter.

I am a very different person than I was before the shelter-in-place time period. I am liking it. In considering an analogy, three months ago, my plans would have been: I am thankful for the world here on the farm that God gave us. Now I need to go someplace else to explore the rest of the world.

I need to go to the ocean. I need to go to the mountains. I need to go on a road trip. I need to experience all these things. This is a big world. I need to explore what He made.

Through being forced to stay right here, it is not a quest anymore. Living here on the farm is my **real** life. I walk outside and appreciate a bird's nest or discover a monarch's egg on a milkweed leaf. There's something new every day.

If I was never able to leave these five acres, I have what I need, along with mail-ordering.

Great is His faithfulness.

Questions to Ponder

1. Ruthmari talks about how scriptural reading in the morning informs her day. How does she describe it? What might an experience like that look like for you?

2. Nature plays a big part in Ruthmari's conversations with God and the gratitude she gives back to Him. How does scripture help you recognize God and His presence around you and in creation?

3. Noticing God in nature also gave Ruthmari peace and rest for her soul. She realized she had all she needed. How does feeling God's presence remove the quest for more? Where do you need assurances of His faithfulness and covering your needs?

Action

What scriptures can hang on your wall or be put on your mirror as reminders every morning?

Scriptural Prayer[18]

Using scripture to frame your awareness, wonder, and requests of God.

Remember, as you face difficulties of any kind, the Lord is ever-present with you. The way to approach your life is through His word.

Ruthmari talked about scripture informing her thoughts throughout the day. That can happen to you as well.

1. Choose a section of Scripture that meets a need of your heart. The following verses can work well.

   "So do not fear, for I am with you; do not be dismayed, for I am your God. I will strengthen you and help you; I will uphold you with my righteous right hand" (Isaiah 41:10 NIV).

2. Ponder what you want to ask God for in your prayer. Then as you repeat it back to Him, add your own personalized style to it. For example,

   Dear God,

   I do not want to fear today. I am so glad You are with me. Help me not be dismayed for I cling to and trust that You are my God. Thank You for strengthening and helping me face _____.

I am so grateful that You are holding me up with Your
righteous right hand and
    I am holding on tightly!
    Amen

3. Review the differences between the prayer in #2 and the scripture in #1. How did the prayer take the words of the verse and make it a personal prayer?

4. When you create your own prayers, based on His words, they begin to sink down into your heart and you can attend to His voice whispering over you.

5. Scriptural prayers embed in your heart and mind, and His words come to your consciousness at just the right time. For example, Ruthmari talked about the scriptures helping her be encouraged by His presence all around her and she had all that she needed.

"The LORD is my shepherd, I lack nothing" (Psalm 23:1 NIV).

6. Other passages you may want to experiment with may include Psalm 23, Deuteronomy 31:8, Jeremiah 29:11, Philippians 4:6–8.

7. Download the free scripture cards (https://NancyBBooth. com/want-to-hear-god) provided as a helpful resource.

Chapter 11

Calling
Intercessory

"I am crying aloud to You, O True God, for I long
to know Your answer. Hear me, O God. Hear my
plea. Hear my prayer for help." Psalm 17:6

Mark

I pray in a different way. I pray as I run.

I listen. I call out to Him like King David did in the Psalms
and feel He talks to me directly as I run. This call and response
keep me praying.

I listen and cry out to God and then become calm.

I feel like I have had that so many times... as I run...

It doesn't happen every time I run. I'll be thinking and praying.

One time, I think it was last week when I was running, God stopped me in my tracks and said something to me: *"Talk to your Facebook friends."*

I'm not a big Facebook person. I'm not good at that. Nor do I want to be. I've gotten burned too many times.

God said, *"Tell them that you love them and that you just want to give them some levity."*

So, I got on Facebook and shared some jokes. So that was God spurring me on. It's really cool. I react to whatever I hear Him saying.

Another time, I was praying for people and God stopped me in my tracks again. I don't know if that is weird. I had gone by the high school in times past and I remember just praying and hearing Him say, *"Pray for the high schoolers right now, they need you."*

So, I stopped at the high school, lifted my hands, and prayed for all the high school kids. I included the ones that are in the youth group I work with.

I was thinking of other times, like Jenny. Two weeks ago, she came to my mind. I prayed. Then, *"You need to text her and make sure she knows that you have prayed for her, whatever she is struggling with."*

That is an example of one of the prayer conversations I have while running.

I want to stay sensitive and be obedient to the thoughts and prompts that I am having, and running aids me in doing that.

Questions to Ponder

1. Mark finds he talks to and connects with God while running. When and where do you find yourself in a place to connect with God? Running, gardening, walking? What activity might you try as you have your conversations with God and who it is you are to be praying for (interceding)?

2. Mark says, *I was praying for people and God stopped me in my tracks. I don't know if that is weird.* Have you felt that way when you detect God is sharing something with you? Often, we don't allow ourselves to talk about our prayer experiences with each other. What "weird" experiences have you had that you could talk over with someone else?

Action

What activity might you choose to be doing to be listening to God interceding? Discover how to do that process in the steps that follow.

Intercessory Prayer

Praying for someone that God reveals to your mind so that you can be a distributor of God's love to them as you pray for them.

1. Come before God in silence.
2. Realize that Jesus is interceding for those you are bringing to Him.

   "From such a vantage, He is able to save those who approach God through Him for all time because He will forever live to be their advocate *in the presence of God.*" Hebrews 7:25

3. Also, know that the Holy Spirit is interceding for whomever He places on your heart. He prays even when you are not sure what to pray.

   "A similar thing happens *when we pray.* We are weak and do not know how to pray, so the Spirit steps in and articulates prayers for us with groaning too profound for words." Romans 8:26

4. As you join with God in prayer, remember you are distributors of His love, not producers. Be the link for people and hold them up to an almighty God, then release them to Him.

5. Ask God who you are to pray and intercede for this day. Wait as names and/or faces appear. This intercession can also occur while you are walking, gardening, or running as in Mark's example.

6. Ask Him, *"What is your prayer for this person?"*

7. Is there anything you need to surrender as you come to God? Give everything to Him as you come.

8. Picture bringing people to God. What might Jesus want to say to you about them? When finished, then leave them with Jesus. Tell Jesus your intent is to leave them with Him, rather than "fix" anything on your own.

9. Commit your interceding efforts to God. Ask Him to use your efforts for His glory and the good of the world. You may even wish to intercede for things of the world, with the newspaper, TV news, or even social media in mind.

10. You can keep a list of who and what you intercede for in the journal provided so you can record how God uses your prayers in distributing His love. Keeping this list can be a fascinating insight into how you are joining God at work.

Chapter 12

Serving
Believers' Prayer

"The eyes of the LORD search the whole earth in order to strengthen those whose hearts are fully committed to him." 2 Chronicles 16:9 NLT

Nancy

I could feel my anxiety rising.

Urbana 18, InterVarsity Fellowship's big college conference gathering, kept getting closer and closer. Who was I to support a team of twenty in prayer and care? This team of twenty who were in charge of the whole operations of this 12,000 people missions conference?

What were you thinking, Lord?

I had been working with the team in prayer and care for the past ten months at their local headquarters, two to three days of meetings per month. However, we were approaching the on-call, nine-day conference when I felt responsible for the team at all hours at the huge American Center in St Louis. I wondered if I was truly up to the challenge.

God, as the creator God that He is, saw me in my dilemma. He connected me to chapter 33 in Exodus. Moses is talking to God after the Israelites had disobeyed Moses and made the golden calf. Moses, in this most intimate conversation with God, wonders out loud to God, *Who am I to lead these people?*

Moses *(to the Lord)*: Look, You tell me, 'Lead these people!' but You haven't yet told me whom You will send to accompany me. Yet You tell me, 'I know you by name, and you have gained My trust and blessing.'

If I have gained Your trust and blessing, reveal Your way to me so that I can truly know You, and so that I may gain Your favor. Remember that this nation is Your *covenant* people.

Eternal One: *My presence will travel with you, and I will give you rest*" (my emphasis, Exodus 33:12–14).

When I read those words, I felt a huge weight come off my shoulders. God is sovereign. He is everywhere. He is going to the conference with me. I am not going alone. I am not totally responsible.

My breath prayer became *"I AM with you,"* knowing God was my great I AM.

He reinforced that concept on the first day of the conference. Starting the day with God in prayer, He impressed on me to find Gloria (not her real name) because she was in distress. When I got over to the arena, I looked for her in her assigned area but to no avail.

After looking in several areas in the huge arena, I walked to the conference center coffee shop, with her still on my heart. As I drank my tea, to my surprise, she came walking into the coffee shop! God brought her to me instead. Such a kind and gracious God.

Indeed, Gloria had had a sleepless night and needed God's word. We prayed His word over her, calming her anxious heart.

God saw her and sent His support to her. I knew then I could trust He would show me the way for the entire conference as I kept open to His nudges.

He showed me His sovereignty and I could trust His hand.

I need only practice His presence.

Questions to Ponder

1. How does seeing God as Creator and Sovereign, ever present, make a difference in Nancy's prayers? How could it make a difference in your prayers?
2. What surprised you in the outcome of Nancy's conversation with God? Have you had conversations with God like this? What would it take to talk with God like this?

Action

How will you react to God's prompting when He places someone on your heart to find and pray for him/her?

Believers' Prayer

A big-picture prayer in service for others, seeing the world as God sees it and asking for only things God can do on behalf of His people, ever aware of His presence.

In Acts 4, the apostle Peter prayed with a crowd of believers. He had been let go from the rulers and elders of the people because of his teaching that Jesus' resurrection from the dead was possible. They violently disagreed with this teaching.

You can utilize these principles of prayer for yourself to bring up big pictures of what God is doing in the world. Or you can gather two or three together to pray for your community, state, country, or world.

In this prayer from Acts 4:24–30, Peter demonstrates four principles to give each of us, as a community of believers, a bigger lens to pray to our awesome God and courage in sharing Jesus. Those principles include:

1. Pray to our Creator God
2. Recognize His sovereignty
3. Ask for courageous confidence
4. Expect Him to answer

Pray to Creator God

Peter prays:

"God, our King, You made the heaven and the earth and the sea and everything they contain. You are the One who, by the Holy Spirit, spoke through our ancestor David, Your servant, with these words:

Why did the nations rage? Why did they imagine useless things? The kings of the earth took their stand; their rulers assembled in opposition against the Eternal One and His Anointed King" (verses 24–26).

Recognize His Sovereignty

Peter recognizes:

"This is exactly what has happened among us, here in this city. The *foreign ruler* Pontius Pilate and the *Jewish ruler* Herod, along with their respective peoples, have assembled in opposition to Your holy servant Jesus, the One You chose. They have done whatever Your hand and plan predetermined should happen" (verses 27–28).

Ask for courageous confidence

He asks:

"And now, Lord, take note of their intimidations *intended to silence us*. Grant us, Your servants, the courageous confidence we need to go ahead and proclaim Your message" (verse 29).

Expect Him to Answer

Then finally verbalizes what he expects:

"[W]hile You reach out Your hand to heal people, enabling us to perform signs and wonders through the name of Your holy servant Jesus" (verse 30).

Application

Now you can use these principles and put them into practice. Hopefully, you can join others in this prayer, as Peter did.

1. As you come to prayer, remember who you are praying to:

    O Creator God, maker of heaven and earth...

    Do whatever you need to do to get in touch with that Creator side of God—nature, night sky, up-close look at flowers and birds, whatever captures your imagination about the magnificence of God as Creator.

2. Also, consider that He is Sovereign, full of power and majesty, without any interference from outside sources, as you seek His face.

    You alone are powerful, majestic, and trustworthy. You see the total picture.

    What power and majesty of God do you want to access as you come to Him in prayer?

3. Ask Him then for courage and wisdom in what to pray for in what you are facing and how to join Him.

    Lord, today, I need your courage and wisdom to persevere in the midst of the chaos across the land. I confess I only want to run and hide. However, You call me to join You in praying for people, to reach out to others as I share Your love and grace, to see justice and mercy come because I am willing to pray, to act, and to share resources in supporting others.

Make your prayer as specific as possible. What is it you need or others need in the situations they are facing?

4. Expect Him to show Himself in miracles and wonders as you step out in faith with Him.

    I will see Your hand at work in the lives of people around me, have divine appointments, and see Your provision as I keep my eyes and ears open and make myself available.

    Thank You, Jesus, for letting me join You where You are working.

    Amen

Don't forget to look for miracles and wonders after you pray. Keep up the prayers, even when you don't see the results.

He will answer in amazing ways. You'll be serving others and distributing His love through your believers' prayers.

Section 4

Your Next Steps with Him

In this last section, you have the opportunity to reflect on the prayer conversations you have had with God.

Where has He been speaking to you?

What transformations have blown you away?

Now what?

Chapter 13

Reflecting Back
Going Forward

"But I have come to give you everything in
abundance, more than you expect—life in its
fullness until you overflow!" John 10:10b TPT

Your Turn

*B*efore *you move forward, take time to reflect on how far you
have come in establishing new connections and conversations
with God.*

In the twelve ways of prayer conversations that you have explored
in this book, set aside some time now to explore, reread your journal,
and reflect on the authentic conversations you have had.

You may wish to find a quiet room of your home, a beautiful
park, or even reserve a room away from home. Do whatever you

need to do to have some silence and solitude for yourself and recognize the journey you have taken.

Reflecting back on the two-way conversations with God

Review the list of prayer practices in the appendix and reflect about which ones helped you have particularly meaningful conversations with God.

1. How have you and God connected in the different two-way conversations?

   Take time to review notes you made in your journal. Where did you feel especially close and intimate with God? What clicked?

2. What authentic prayer conversations *do you want to continue* to explore with Him?

   As you look back at your journal, there may be prayer practices that motivate you, excite you, even noticing prayer conversations you want more of or you'd like to repeat. Reflect upon those special prayer conversations. What abundance have you noticed growing or want to grow?

3. What is your heart's desire?

   Sometimes it takes time to filter through the myriad of thoughts and emotions to drill down to the true heart desires. At this point in your life:

   What are you desiring from God? Peace, joy, freedom, significance...

   What is He desiring from you? Ask Him and keep asking until you feel clarity.

Going forward in two-way conversations and connections with God

The next part of continuing your conversations with God is up to you. He will continue to speak to you if that is what you desire.

Using your imagination can be a powerful tool. Picture yourself on a path, walking with Jesus. Where are you walking? See yourself in a conversation with Him.

What kinds of conversations and connections do You want to have with me, Jesus?

I hope you take time to ponder, listen for His voice, and see yourself speaking to Him. He will provide purpose, wisdom, and clarity for deepening your life-long intimate relationship with Him.

Now to action

You have dreamed with God and Jesus, listened for His voice, and asked Him for guidance. How do you now put that into action?

In the appendix is an outline for setting yourself up for action. The same page is also in the journal you downloaded earlier.

In order to enjoy hearing God and connecting with Him in prayer, I believe in establishing a regular habit of listening and hearing God. This prayer habit can bring the abundance Jesus mentions in John 10:10. To establish a habit requires an intentional plan.

James Clear, in his book *Atomic Habits* suggests how to build new habits. There are four practices to help the habits to stick. The habit must be obvious, attractive, easy, and satisfying. By making your prayer conversations with God meet those requirements, you establish rich, abundant habit-forming prayer times and enjoy intimate conversations that transform.

So, have God help you put your intentions into place and determine how you might form new habits for meeting with God going forward.

1. *How can your prayer conversations become obvious in your life?*
   By becoming obvious, you establish a cue every time you see a space or do an activity. That cue or trigger announces it is time to talk to God.

For example, find a cozy, inviting place to meet with God so that every time you pass that place, you'll want to stop there to pray. Or perhaps you have an activity that each time you see or do it, like running or working in your garden, you're cued to easily talk to God. Whatever you choose will be a cue or trigger to remind you, "Oh, I get to talk with God, now."

My obvious cue to talk to God will be _____.

2. *How will prayer conversations become attractive to you so that you crave time with God?*

Often stacking a habit with another one will help you be attracted to get moving on a new habit. For example, enjoying your morning cup of coffee prompts you and even can set up a craving to have a conversation with God. For me, it's my early morning diet coke, before I look at my phone feed. What could be something you enjoy doing that prompts make the meeting with God irresistible?

My irresistible movement to meeting with God will be

_____.

3. *How can prayer conversations become easier for you?*

Even responding with two minutes in one of the twelve practices you've read about can bring momentum and abundance into your life. Responding to that irresistible moment with God gets the ball rolling. Which prayer practice response could you prepare to easily bring two minutes of God into your life daily?

My beginning two-minute prayer practice response will be _____.

4. *How can you track the God conversations and activity in your life?*

Finally, the most satisfying thing about establishing a habit of meeting with God is seeing Him at work in your life on a daily basis. His response to your prayers is so rewarding. Get a small calendar to track your meetings with Him. Check off each day to build momentum and develop a daily habit of conversing with Him. Your brain will pick up on that little daily awareness of God's presence in your day-to-day living. Tracking even one prayer practice and God sightings daily will help you hear God's voice and bring discernment into your life as well as a sense of awe. What can you use to track your daily meeting with God?

My daily meetings with God will be tracked by

_____.

By incorporating prayer conversations that are obvious, attractive, easy, and satisfying, you'll develop abundant prayer conversations. Even in a noisy, distracting, busy world, you will hear God, connect with Him in prayer, and have intimate conversations that transform your life.

Praying for you

My final prayer for you is based on Ephesians 3:18 TPT.

My Friends,
I pray that you will discover
How deeply intimate and far-reaching is Jesus' love!
Endless love beyond measurement
May His extravagant, abundant love pour into you until you are
filled to overflowing with the fullness of God!
May you have endless conversations that fill your soul.
Amen and Amen
I will be praying for you, my friends!
In Jesus' love,

Nancy B Booth

Setting Up Your Next Steps

Plan of Action: Habits to Develop

Prayer practices I found enjoyable:

My obvious cue or reminder to talk to God will be:

My irresistible movement to meeting with God will be:

My beginning two-minute prayer practice response will be:

I want to enjoy seeing God at work through our conversations so I will track our daily conversations by:

Prayer Practices

Jesus says, *I came to give life with joy and abundance. John 10:10b*

Creating time to have conversations with Him for a variety of reasons and in a variety of ways can be a place to start. Below you find the index to the prayer practices in this book.

As you read *Want to Hear God, Connect with Him in Prayer* may these pages serve as a reference for you to connect to His life with joy and abundance.

SECTION 1		
Empower Your Present	**Prayer Practice**	**This practice allows you to**
Being present	Breath	Take a short breath phrase with you throughout your day, based on your breath.
Experiencing	Lectio Divina	Read scripture through 3 different questions that allow God to speak to your heart.
Seeing	Examen	Review your day, seeing where you were close to God and where you felt you were far away.
Sensing	Centering	Meditate 10–20 minutes by listening to God without words.

SECTION 2		
Redeem Your Past	**Prayer Practice**	**This practice allows you to**
Surrender	Confession	Confess your wrongdoings, ask forgiveness and make a new start.
Grieving	Lament	Cry out to God with all emotions, tell Him like it is, and focus on who He is.
Healing	Imaginary	Place yourself within Jesus' healing touch.
Resting	Silence/Solitude	Meditate and lean into God's word in silence.

SECTION 3		
Change Your Future	**Prayer Practice**	**This practice allows you to**
Praising	Gratitude	Practice daily thanking God in all things.
Asking	Scripture	Using scripture to frame your requests to God.
Calling	Intercessory	Learn to listen for who you are to pray and intercede for.
Serving	Believers'	Know how to serve and pray for other believers.

SECTION 4	
Live in His Presence	
Reflecting	Review the 12 practices.
Going Forward	Make a habit-forming plan of action.

Gratitudes

First of all, I give God the main praise. This book looks nothing like I started with and I want to give Him all the glory. I am beyond thankful for the way He has directed me, past and present, to shape this book. He indeed longs for each of us to know we are His beloved.

I have traveled this journey with God and great preachers along the way to establish a firm footing in the scriptures. Thank you, Pastor Gilbert Beenken, Pastor Brad Smith, and Pastor Jeff Lovell. I am greatly indebted to your love of Jesus and the Scriptures.

I discovered two-way conversations with God when I started my spiritual direction training with incredible mentors Marty and Sandy Boller through Sustainable Faith. My first spiritual director, Mary Yerkes, helped me hear God speak and heal my heart.

God knew I needed support to write this book. He connected me with Shelley and CJ Hitz at Christian Book Academy. Their enthusiasm, knowledge of writing, and love of Jesus have made this book possible. They certainly knew how to encourage writing with my "priestly pen." CBA also connected me with Debra Butterfield, whose expertise in editing and formatting gives this book the look it deserves when sharing about God.

The impact of InterVarsity and Urbana 2018 under the leadership of Matt Rust showed me how I could indeed partner with God, hear His voice clearly, and practice His presence in serving others.

Finally, this book would not be completed without the help of the friends who prayed for this book and agreed to share their prayers and conversations with me. My heartfelt thanks go out to the contributors, Amy, Deanne, Cheri, Matt, Rayna, Sheri, Jeff, Mary, Mark, and Ruthmari (read about them in the contributors section.) Sharing your sacred moments of conversation and connection with God has shown others how they, too, can hear God speak to them.

Thank you, too, for other praying friends: Jennifer, Cathy, Jan, Doris, Debi, Cam, Chelsea, Marty, Sandy, Kim, Cheryl, Christian Book Academy friends, Ezra friends and my family. You have been generous with your encouragement and commitment to pray this book into fruition.

With God's blessings, this will be the first of a series of books featuring prayer conversations that transform. I believe sharing the conversations we have with God encourages each of us and strengthens our faith.

I will be praying for you, the reader, as you gather with others, explore the prayer conversations in this book, and share your own conversations you've had with God.

He wants to connect with you. I am certain of that.

Blessings,

Nancy B Booth

March 2021

Endnotes

1. Kim Avery, *The Prayer-Powered Entrepreneur* (New York: Morgan James Publishing, 2020).

2. Nancy Booth, Medium, "Prayer Can Be As Easy As Breathing," https://medium.com/publishous/prayer-can-be-as-easy-as-breathing-b8938050a94f?source=friends_link&sk=f8c52fa-ca507a7bcda2ab59e341b67bd.

3. Mary Kate Morse, *A Guidebook to Prayer* (Downers Grove, IL: Intervarsity Press, 2013), 126.

4. Adele & Doug Calhoun, Clare & Scott Loughrige, *Spiritual Rhythms for the Enneagram, A Handbook for Harmony and Transformation* (Downers Grove, IL: Intervarsity Press, 2019), 205-207.

5. Reimagining the Examen, https://www.ignatianspirituality.com/reimagining-examen-app/

6. Adele Ahlberg Calhoun, *Spiritual Disciplines Handbook, Practices That Transform Us* (Downers Grove, IL: Intervarsity Press, 2005), 205.

7. Centering Prayer App, https://www.contemplativeoutreach.org/

centering-prayer-mobile-app

8. Brené Brown, "Brené on Anxiety, Calm +Over/Under-Functioning," *Unlocking Us* Podcast, April 3, 2020, https://brenebrown.com/podcast/brene-on-anxiety-calm-over-under-functioning/.

9. Donna Jones, "What is Confessional Prayer and How Do You Pray It?" April 26, 2019, https://www.crosswalk.com/faith/prayer/what-is-a-confession-prayer.html.

10. Christina Fox, "The Way of Lament," May 5, 2016, https://www.ligonier.org/blog/way-lament/.

11. Rayna Neises Life and Leadership Coach, Lament process adapted from Take Heart Coaching, https://www.takeheartcoaching.com.

12. Ignatian exercises, https://www.ignatianspirituality.com/ignatian-prayer/the-spiritual-exercises/.

13. Beth and Dave Booram, *When Faith Becomes Sight, Opening Your Eyes to God's Presence All Around You* (Downers Grove, IL: Intervarsity Press, 2019), 78-90.

14. NIV Dramatized, Luke 10:38–42, https://www.biblegateway.com/passage/?search=Luke%2010%3A38-42&version=NIV.

15. Dallas Willard, *quoted in*, Ruth Haley Barton, *Invitation to Solitude and Silence, Experiencing God's Transforming Presence* (Downers Grove, IL: Intervarsity Press, 2010), 11.

16. Ruth Haley Barton, *Invitation to Retreat, The Gift and Necessity of Time Away with God,* (Downers Grove, IL: Intervarsity Press, 2018), 116.

17. Melody Beattie, *Make Miracles in Forty Days: Turning What You Have into What You Want,* (New York: Simon & Schuster, 2010), 35–61.

18. Adelle Ahlberg Calhoun, *Spiritual Disciplines Handbook, Practices That Transform Us,* (Downers Grove, IL: InterVarsity Press, 2005), 245

Welcoming Jesus Into Your Life

How well do you know Jesus? A relationship with Him is your key to hearing God and having that intimate relationship in prayer you desire.

Jesus says in John 15:14. NLT, "You are my friends if you do what I command."

So you ask, "How do I get to be a friend of Jesus? What is it He commands?"

To welcome Jesus into your life as a friend, you need to realize how much and often you "miss the mark," or sin.

"Since we've compiled this long and sorry record as sinners (both us and them) and proved that we are utterly incapable of living the glorious lives God wills for us, God did it for us. Out of sheer generosity, he put us in right standing with himself.

103

A pure gift. He got us out of the mess we're in and restored us to where he always wanted us to be. And he did it by means of Jesus Christ". Romans 3:23–24 MSG

It is by believing in Jesus and all the work He did for us — dying for our sins on the cross and rising from the dead—that we can now be connected and in right standing with God.

By being a friend of Jesus, you and I are now forgiven. The past is forgotten and we have a new life, both now and forever. What an amazing gift!

If you have never welcomed Jesus into your life, now is the time to ask Him to forgive you and become your Savior and friend. I am praying for your connection with Him.

Take time to pray the following prayer:

God,

I do know you love me. I know that I am a sinner and miss the mark so many times. I know that You sent Jesus to die on the cross and cover my sins. Jesus is now risen and can be my friend and Savior. I am overwhelmed by that gift of sacrifice. I accept Your gift of love. Thank you that I can now be forgiven and connected to You and Jesus, now and forever.

In Jesus name,

Amen

May Jesus continue to grow and be a real friend in your life!

Contributors

 I am Amy. I love gathering people together. It might be in a yoga class or around a campfire or on the porch with a cup of coffee, but my favorite place is around the table! Whether it's with my growing family with grands or friends, there's always room for one more. And if we need to, we'll build a bigger table!

 I am Deanne Welsh, a marketing maverick, copywriter, storyteller, and author. I equip my clients to share their stories and art with magnetic messaging and a powerful online presence. I also coach writers on finally finishing and self-publishing their books. I am the author of four books, including my most recent release *Adrift: True Stories of a Modern Mermaid*, about growing up on ships that sailed around the world.

I am Cheri, a spiritual director in the Dallas/Ft Worth area and beyond, via Zoom. Learning various ways to pray and teaching those ways to others has been my vocation since 2009. I have recently become a grandmother, the best new role ever.

I am Matt, married to my best friend, Lisa. With four amazing sons and one daughter-in-law. At this moment I am most likely either reading, watching baseball, listening to music, or pondering what it means to be, as Carlos Carretto writes, "Thunderstruck at the mystery of Christ's incarnation."

I am Nancy Booth, author, Jesus lover, certified life coach, and spiritual director. My passion is to create ways for women and men to connect with God and Jesus through personal prayer that leads to a life Jesus calls "abundant." I live in southern Wisconsin in a beautiful oak grove, with my husband, Jim of forty-plus years. We enjoy visits with our adult children and four delightful grandchildren who bring joy and giggles to our lives.

I am Rayna Neises, author, certified coach, host of *A Season of Caring* Podcast, and speaker who is passionate about supporting women and men who are in a season of caring for aging parents. I lost both of my parents to Alzheimer's Disease. After my season for caring for my dad through his journey, I founded A Season of Caring Coaching where I equip, encourage, and support those in this season. I don't want them to aimlessly wander through this important season of life. I live on a farm in southeast Kansas with my husband, Ron, and a small pack of dogs. I enjoy crafts of all kinds and spending time with my grandkids most of all.

I am Sheri, a life-long pilgrim of this world, formed and transformed by God and the people and events that have graced my life. I have an open mind and heart for the way God (however you come to see your image of God) works among all people. Personally, I have experienced the power of redemption in a cycle known as the "death and resurrection" of Jesus Christ. This power is found in learning to live in a surrendered position before God, humble and ready to be available when needed. I don't try to save the world anymore. I try to live my life in this beautiful rhythm of grace, knowing that God brings all things together for the greater good!

I am Jeff, a pastor and coach for leaders in Wisconsin with a vision to help churches and communities thrive. I currently serve as the lead pastor at Ezra Church in Stoughton, Wisconsin. When I am not helping leaders grow, you'll likely find me drinking coffee, enjoying time with my wife, or cheering on my daughters at a cross country or swim meet.

I am Mary, a retired special education teacher and past Indiana State President of NAMI, the National Association of Mental Illness. I love reading both fiction and non-fiction and taking long walks with my husband. You'll often find me volunteering in social justice groups. I teach courses on faith and racial healing.

I am Ruthmari, a child of God who takes great delight in His natural creation. I prefer up-close observations and details. It is nearly impossible for me to take a walk and not come home with a pocket full of treasures! My joy is to co-create with God in tending the earth in my gardens and then taking inspiration from that into my studio. I am a jewelry and pottery artist, and my work is influenced greatly by the beauty and intricacies of organic materials. I am grateful for a husband who shares this journey with me. I wish to encourage those around me to slow down and enjoy the simple things of life. My hope is to leave a legacy of this appreciation for my children and grandchildren who have captured my heart.

I am Mark. I am a teacher by career and a lifetime chaser of God. At times it feels like I run away because I got this life, and at most times I run into His embrace. I enjoy praying as I run through the streets of Stoughton, Wisconsin, where I live, and get outside as much as possible. I am a father of two beautiful teenagers and have an amazing wife who I get to call my best friend.

Author Page

Nancy Booth passionately desires to have you hear God speak to you, His beloved. As a Jesus lover and spiritual director, she walks alongside mid-lifers seeking encounters with God. She supports you in finding clarity and connections with God and the abundant life that can bring.

Just as Jesus healed the woman in the crowd when she touched His hem, Nancy has experienced the healing touch of Jesus in her own life by being healed from depression and anxiety.

Nancy enjoys her life in southern Wisconsin with her husband, Jim, of over forty-five years, their grown children, and their four delightful grandchildren that bring light, joy, and giggles into their lives.

Abundant Grace
Publishers

If you enjoyed this book, consider sharing it with others.

- Please mention the book on Facebook, Twitter, Pinterest, or your blog.

- Recommend this book to your small groups, book club, and workplace.

- Head over to Facebook.com/**NancyBBooth**, "Like" the page and post a comment as to what you enjoyed the most.

- Pick up a copy for someone you know who would be challenged or encouraged by this message.

- Write a review on Goodreads or a platform of your choice.

NOTES

Made in the USA
Las Vegas, NV
17 May 2021

23195341R00066